COME HOME
WE LOVE YOU STILL

JUSTIN GRIMBOL

ATLATL

Atlatl Press
POB 293161
Dayton, Ohio 45429
atlatlpress.com

COME HOME

WE LOVE YOU STILL

"CAN YOU HEAR the loons?"

"Yes, I can. They sound like they are up to no good."

"I love that sound. Don't you love that sound?"

"I do. Loons are great. I would snuggle with one if I could."

"Sexually?"

"Is there any other way?"

"I don't know."

"Hey, you know what I just realized?"

"What?"

"I don't even know what a loon looks like."

"Shut up."

"Seriously, I don't have a clue what they look like. They could look like humans. Big old naked humans hanging out at a lake butt naked. Wouldn't that be creepy?"

"It doesn't matter."

"It doesn't?"

"No. Just listen to them. They're amazing."

"How DID ALL these bugs get into the cabin?"

"The door."

"Will they eat us in our sleep?"

"They may nibble on us a bit."

"That doesn't bother you?"

"No."

"Well, it bothers me."

"I know it does. You hate bugs."

"I'm a light sleeper."

"The lightest."

"I heard the loons again last night."

"I love the loons. How were the loons?"

"I think they were having a loon fight."

"They were?"

"I think so. They were being really loud."

"I'm getting sleepy."

"I don't trust these bugs."

"I'm so tired. Let's go to sleep now. Okay?"

"Maybe I should kill them all."

"That would be nice. Goodnight, baby."

"I really want to kill these fucking things. It might take a while. But it would be worth it."

"WHAT ARE YOU going to do today?"

"I need to shower."

"Then shower."

"I'm gonna."

"Use soap. Wash your butt."

"I always do."

"Wash your dick too."

"SHE'S MY DOG."

"No, she's my dog."

"If we get divorced, the dog will be mine."

"Untrue. She's mine. WHEN we get divorced, she will live with me."

"Nope. She is my sweet pit bull puppy."

"If she went with you the poor girl would never walk again."

"I just don't think the dog could handle all your nagging and guilt tripping."

"She's my dog!"

"Should we double snuggle her?"

"A snuggle from both sides?"

"Yes."

"Let's do it."

"Gross. You have boogers in your beard."

"They have always been there."

"No they haven't. You just sneezed into your beard. Like an animal."

"I'm sick. I can't help myself."

"THESE MILLENNIALS ARE a bunch of Muppet Babies."

"But YOU are a millennial."

"I know. I'm a Muppet Baby too. But I'm more like a big Muppet Baby that's been left outside in the rain. That's me. That's what I am like."

"You know which Muppet you remind me of?"

"Which one?"

"The purple one. The purple dinosaur."

"Barney?"

"Yeah, that one."

"Barney is not a Muppet or a baby."

"You are such a know-it-all."

"Our love affair has spanned generations."

"Shut up, you aren't that much older than me."

"I'm an old soul though."

"Your soul needs adult-sized diapers. Your soul needs Ze-absorb."

"My soul needs to take its pills."

"Why won't you watch this movie with me?"

"What's it about?"

"Bunny rabbits."

"Well there you have it. I'm a full grown adult, and I don't want to watch a movie about bunny rabbits."

"But it's beautiful. It's a really sad movie."

"I do like to watch you cry."

"You like to ruin beautiful moments."

"No, that's not it. Your man tears are just really entertaining."

"They inspire people."

"Yeah, right."

"They will change the world one day."

"HONEY, YOU LOOK adorable in that bathing suit. But you can't swim now. The cops are here and they told everyone they can't swim under the waterfall."

"Really?"

"I know it's so totally lame."

"This can't be happening."

"I'm sorry, baby."

"I was really looking forward to swimming under that waterfall."

"I know."

"I watched everyone else swim. Then I went to the bathroom to change into my bathing suit and I come back out and now nobody is allowed to swim anymore."

"The cop kicked everyone out of the water."

"But YOU got to swim."

"I know. The cops weren't here before. It was lawless. I got to frolic with college kids that have just graduated and have high hopes for the future and stuff."

"I watched the dog while you swam."

"That was really nice of you."

"You got to swim for a really long time."

"I know. It was invigorating. It was mind, body, spirit, and all that stuff. I lounged under a big waterfall. It was the best time ever. But that was then. And this is now. The cops have come and broken the whole thing up. We are not allowed to swim here anymore."

"But I want to go swimming too."

"I know."

"This really sucks."

"Don't be upset."

"I am upset. I deserve to be upset."

"Let's find another waterfall to swim under. This place has so many fucking waterfalls. Let's just find a new one."

"No. I wanted to swim here."

"I know, baby. I know you did."

"This sucks. Everyone knows I like to swim the most. I like to swim more than anybody else."

"Baby, it's not that big of a deal."

"DON'T TELL ME IT'S NOT A BIG DEAL!"

"You're right. It is a pretty big deal. Sorry."

"I'm mad at you."

"I know."

"I worshiped God when I was zero years old."

    "You were probably a really cute zero-year-old."

    "My mom tells me I cried all the time before I was born."

    "Even when you were in her belly?"

    "Even before I was in the belly."

    "Doesn't that just mean your mom was crying?"

    "No, that is not how it works."

"This town has too much weather."

"And pizza."

"And there's a strip club right on Main Street."

"It's the only chill bar in town. The rest of them are packed with college kids. College kids who don't read or feel sappy-hearted enough of the time."

"I miss the bars in Racine, Wisconsin."

"They were better. Better mozzarella sticks and fish fries."

"I wish upstate New York and Wisconsin could dry hump unprotected. And have a baby."

"Yup. Just like my parents."

"Your dad is so Midwestern. Your mom was from here, right? Was your mom very upstate New York-ish?"

"I don't know. I assume so. That's what I am trying to figure out by moving here, and stealing the shade of these pine trees."

"I had a feeling that's what was going on."

"Ghosts are lonely. Especially when you visit them."

"Ghosts can only dry hump, because they have no insides."

"I CAN'T WAIT for the public pool to open. I'm going to do awesome cannonball jumps off the diving board."

"It's going to be amazing. I'm so glad we have the pool right down the street. It's so nice there. Surrounded by pine trees and you can hear the creek."

"It's really peaceful. But we can't bring the dog."

"Shit, you're right. Maybe we can dress the dog up in a coat and hat so everyone will think she's a human."

"But you can't go swimming in a coat and hat."

"Good point."

"Besides, dogs hate being dressed up like that."

"I WANT TO wear more sweatpants."

"Well, we have a problem then, because I want you to wear less sweatpants, or to give up on sweatpants altogether."

"I could imagine switching to bathing trunks. But I don't like the mesh lining. They make my funky dunky feel caged."

"As it should."

"I'M WORRIED WE are using our credit card too often. I think we need to cut down. Use it more sparingly."

"I say we use it as often as possible. Maxing out your credit cards is an important part of being an adult."

"We were supposed to use it for emergencies only. Now we use it whenever we want pizza."

"Pizza is an emergency to me."

"Can we try to not use our card so often?"

"Of course. I got a huge jar full of change. We can pretend it's a pirate treasure. It will be fun."

"How much change do you think we have?"

"Enough to last us a lifetime. Or at least a week. And after that, we can use Monopoly money."

"IF I CRY in the morning, I might actually be able to get some decent writing done."

"That sounds like fun. What else did you do today?"

"My dad called. I talked to him for a while."

"How's he doing?"

"Okay, I guess. I told him I wanted to walk across the country. Everyone knows walking three thousand miles is the best weight loss plan ever."

"Unless you die."

"That's funny. He said the same thing."

"And that makes you sad?"

"Sure."

"Why?"

"'Cause."

"He loves you."

"He hates my adventurous spirit."

"Your dad just wants us to stop moving so much."

"I know. Everyone wants us to stop moving and having adventures."

"I don't know about everyone. There's a lot of people out there. Like billions."

"People think we move too much."

"That's true."

"I'm tired of it."

"They want us to grow roots somewhere. Have kids."

"Roots?"

"Yeah, roots."

"They want me to just all of a sudden shoot a million roots out of my ass."

"Something like that."

"Fucking roots."

"Roots aren't bad."

"I guess."

"What's so wrong with roots?"

"Roots are tricky. Some people say they want roots, but then they just live in a place for ten years or so then they move."

"So? That's normal."

"It's normal. But that's not having roots. Roots should mean more than that. You have to live somewhere for way longer than that to grow roots."

"Who are you? The root inspector?"

"I'm just saying. In my not so humble opinion, to have roots you have to live in a place and never leave. You have to have kids there. Those kids gotta have kids. To have roots you either have grandkids that live in the same town as you. Or you got grandparents that live there. And that's only the beginning of roots. Just living in a place for a while isn't having roots."

"Calm down."

"I am calm."

"No, you're not."

"Am too. I'm the most calm. Look how calm I am."

"You are ridiculous."

"I'm calm, God damn it."

"Don't you ever want to settle down one day?"

"Of course."

"Don't you like the idea of having roots, raising some bratty kids? Some chubby, cigarette smoking, goofball children? Then don't you want to see those children raise children in the same town?"

"Of course, but how can you be sure your kids will want to stick around some grumpy little town and raise their kids there?"

"We brainwash them. We brainwash them and blackmail them."

"I'm into that. Just as long as we do it in a loving way."

"It's completely beautiful outside and you know what? I don't give a shit."

"So what are you trying to say?"

"I don't know. I just took such a massive poop."

"We could go for a short hike."

"Maybe. Just give me some time to think it over."

"Have all the time in the world."

"Hey, look at that, you made the bed."

"Damn skippy."

"That's like the third time you have ever done that."

"I'm an adult."

"You are old."

"So old."

"You are old as time."

"I got man boobs."

"You have quite a set."

"That's for certain."

"They're big."

"They're a good size."

"They are as big as time."

"Father Time?"

"Yup."

"Father Time had man boobs?"

"He did."

"That's cool."

"He had man boobs and they looked just like mine."

"WE FIGHT ALL the time."

"No, we fight even more than all the time."

"We fight too much."

"I don't think we fight enough."

"Maybe we should fight less."

"Okay."

"I just don't get it. Why do we fight so fucking much?"

"'Cause you are a defensive person."

"Well, you're a stubborn person."

"You are just as stubborn, if not more."

"I've never met anyone who is so determined to be right all the time."

"Bullshit. I have admitted to being wrong so many times. And I am amazing at apologies. You suck at apologies."

"Here we go again."

"I apologized on twelve separate occasions yesterday. How many times did you apologize?"

"I don't know. I didn't keep track."

"There. I'm the winner of the fight by default. Now you owe me an apology."

"Fuck off."

"See, I told you you suck at apologies."

"I JUST DON'T think old movies are funny."

"You are making me so sad right now."

"The humor in old movies is just so outdated. And awkward. And boring."

"Humor can't be outdated. Something that is truly funny can make all things laugh, forever."

"What are you talking about?"

"The world will end with one great joke that will make everyone that has ever existed laugh and everything will keep laughing for all of existence. God and nothingness will exist in the void and God will be like 'knock, knock,' and the nothingness will be like 'who's there?' That's how everything started, with a great knock knock joke. Humor can't be outdated."

"That's not true."

"You're just obsessed with new things because you wish you were still young."

"Why did you have to go there? Don't you think that's a little harsh? You just really hurt my feelings."

"I'm sorry (see I apologized). You just have to understand. I don't want to watch new movies all the time. They just aren't as interesting. We are going to start having to watch movies separately."

"No, we can't do that. That's too much like divorce. I'll watch some old movies with you."

"You say that, but you never actually do it. Every time I try and watch an old movie, you have a hissy fit."

"We just watched *Fried Green Tomatoes*. That's an old movie. And I loved it."

"That doesn't count as old."

"It's from the fuckin' '90s."

"I want to watch movies from the '70s, the golden age of film."

"This is the golden age of you being pretentious and boring."

"Touché. That was a good line. I'm glad you are funny. You being funny makes fighting feel a lot more worthwhile."

"Thanks. I like your funniness too."

"Now let's watch *M*A*S*H*. It's supposed to be a classic."

"NEVER!"

"Come on. Be fair."

"Can't we just watch *Roseanne* or something?"

"Okay. That's a fair compromise."

"I THINK WE should visit Sag Harbor. I can tell you are homesick."

"I am. I'm a nostalgic guy. Half of me lives in the past."

"Is that healthy?"

"Nothing's healthy."

"You know what I mean."

"I think the trick is, when you visit your past, remembering you are just a ghost there, you can never really interact with it."

"What do you mean?"

"You are a ghost to your own past."

"I still don't get it."

"You can't fight with people in your memories. Or dry hump. Or anything. All you can do is watch it all and haunt what you need to haunt."

"I just think we should go and hang out with your cousin and maybe get a sandwich at Espressos and go to the ocean."

"That would be nice."

"We really should do that."

"We really should. Sandwiches and beaches are awesome. Only I think Espressos is closed."

"You're not wearing pants or underwear."

"I'm not allowed to anymore."

"Says who?"

"I don't know. Sometimes we have to do what we have to do."

"Here we go again."

"Hey, don't give me such a hard time. I had trouble sleeping last night."

"I know you did. I woke up at one point in the middle of the night and you were just staring at me. You looked scary."

"That's 'cause I love you."

"Yeah right."

"I'm a full grown adult love maker."

"Are you?"

"I'm maybe the most romantic person ever."

"Is that so?"

"You wanna do stuff?"

"Stuff in bed?"

"Naked stuff."

"Sure."

"Actually, I changed my mind."

"You did? Already?"

"I did. I changed it. I'm going to put pants on now."

"Don't do that. We should do stuff."

"Oh now you want me to stay pantsless?"

"Well, yeah, I think we should do stuff."

"'Cause we are boyfriend and girlfriend?"

"No, 'cause we are married people."

"Oh. Right. I forgot about that."

"WE SHOULD CHOP trees down for exercise."

"Using what?"

"We will use whatever it is people use to do such things."

"Like?"

"Like choppers."

"Choppers?"

"Or we could use Tai Chi. Just move our bodies like a slight breeze... then... bam! Trees fall down. Exercise achieved. Sweaty muscles. The whole deal."

"I think we should just focus on a more balanced diet and try not to consume so many calories."

"You ruin everything. For a moment there, exercising seemed fun."

"Look at me. Look at my butt."

"Please stop."

"I thought you would like this. I thought it would turn you on. Look at me. I'm like a big naked kitty cat."

"Come on. Stop. I'm eating dinner right now."

"Can I have some of that dinner? I'm just a hungry little STD ridden kitty cat."

"Fuck off a little please. Stop trying to lick my dinner. Stop shaking your butt. Stop making that smell happen."

"I feel like our relationship is going stale. I feel like we don't do enough things."

"Why? Because I don't want to a big naked cat person pestering me while eating spaghetti and meatballs?"

"I just feel like we have lost our zest for doing stuff. Sexy stuff."

"We can do stuff. Just give me like an hour to digest all this food."

"All the spontaneity is gone. I grieve for the lover I once was."

"You got to be kidding me."

"I'm not kidding. You know how sexually sensitive I am."

"Stop. Dear lord. You are being so difficult right now."

"You know what?"

"What?"

"I'm over it."

"You are?"

"I'm fully over it."

"You sure? 'Cause you are still naked and walking around on all fours."

"Doesn't matter. I'm over it. I don't want to have sex anymore. I just want to watch YouTube videos of nerds reviewing things."

"We could have sex in a little bit. I'm almost finished."

"Nope. I'm retired for the evening."

"You want to do it right now?"

"Nope."

"Oh come on. You know how much reverse psychology turns me on."

"I know it does. But this isn't reverse psychology. This is how I truly feel."

"Now you are really getting me horny. Let's do it. Let's do it in bed right now."

"No way. I'm so far from being in the mood."

"Please. This whole massive naked kitty cat thing is actually kinda hot."

"No. I just feel like being alone right now."

"But I want to cuddle and do stuff."

"Nope."

"Please."

"Okay. I guess we can do stuff. If you really want to."

"Can we shower first?"

"Never. You know I hate clean bodies."

"I KINDA WANNA see the new X Men movie."

"Then go see it."

"But I spend so much time hating super hero movies. I'll look like a hypocrite if I go."

"Nobody has to know. It can be our little secret."

"But what if I want to write a dialogue poem about it?"

"Just change the story a little. Make it seem like I was the one that wanted to see the movie."

"But I purposefully make the dialogues confusing. It's hard to tell which one of us is speaking at times. What if I try to make it sound like you are the one going to the lame ass super hero movie, but they think it's me."

"That would be awful."

"I know."

"When does the movie start?"

"In five minutes."

"You should leave now, or you will be late."

"Will you come with me?"

"Hell no."

"Please."

"I said no."

"Fuck, it's too late to go anyway. It looks like I am going to have to stay home and watch boils getting lanced on YouTube."

"I THINK DOGS definitely have souls. When we went on that hike and found that pond surrounded by wildflowers, she got just as excited as we were."

"I think she was even more excited than we were."

"She loved it so much. She ran around so fast."

"She saw the flowers and the tall grass and she wanted it to touch her belly. There were probably so many smells there. She loves to smell things."

"Do you think she has a soul?"

"It depends. What do you think a soul is?"

"I don't think it's anything that complicated."

"I don't either."

"It's HARD TO get used to the way your face looks."

"I shaved it. I shaved the whole thing."

"You just went around and back down and all over the place with that buzzer."

"I might have lost my mind a little bit. Now I'm all shaved up. And I look like a turtle."

"You do look like a turtle."

"I cried about it for a bit."

"You cried more than a bit. You were naked, bald and sobbing. It was intense."

"A little weird."

"Now you are acting so casual about it."

"It's important to act casual about intense things."

"I guess."

"I'm glad we went on that hike. That calmed me down so much. Centered the fuck out of me."

"Nature is good medicine."

"It's nasal spray for the soul."

"Should I come to the vet with you?"

"I don't know."

"I'm just trying to be supportive."

"That's sweet. But the vet makes you so anxious. And then you say weird things?"

"It's true."

"Remember when you asked the vet if you had anal glands?"

"I was curious."

"I just think you should stay here."

"Okay."

"I CAN'T BELIEVE our puppy might have cancer."

"She's not really a puppy. She's like three years old."

"That's still so young."

"Just remember. We don't know anything yet for sure. The results from the biopsy don't come back until Monday."

"I don't have a good feeling about this."

"What did the vet sound like when you talked to her?"

"She sounded like a vet."

"What does that mean?"

"I don't fucking know."

"Come on, work with me here."

"She was worried. She said she didn't know what else it could be."

"Shit. Sometimes I think we love her too much."

"We are addicted to her. We might be too attached."

"Are we being crazy?"

"No. She's the best dog ever. We're just like this."

"Like what?"

"We're sappy."

"And sensitive."

"We get attached."

"So attached."

"We cry easily."

"Well, you cry easily."

"Right."

"It's true."

"I know."

"You cry way more than me."

"You made your point."

"Sorry."

"I can't believe she might have puppy cancer."

"What's that?"

"Cancer of the puppy."

"That's adorable."

"I love her little almond shaped eyes and her little white paws."

"You okay?"

"I don't think so."

"We are going to be okay."

"I keep trying to remind myself that puppies aren't supposed to live forever."

"Me too."

"This isn't the worst thing that can happen."

"I know."

"It's not like one of us got paralyzed."

"Or like one of us has cancer."

"Do you think our landlord will let us get a new dog if she dies?"

"I hope so."

"Are you going to write about this?"

"What do you mean?"

"Are you going to turn it into one of your dialogue poems?"

"I don't think so. I want to keep this private. Maybe later. Maybe in a bunch of years."

"It would make for pretty sappy dialogue."

"It would. I don't think it would work."

"Maybe it would."

"No, I am going to avoid writing about it."

"What about this one?"

"This one? The one we are writing right now?"

"Yes."

"I will use this one."

"So you will write about it."

"Can we not argue?"

"I'm not arguing. Not on purpose, at least."

"I will use this one."

"Which one?"

"You know."

"No, I have no idea."

"This one. The one we are in right now."

"Oh, that one."

"Yes."

"That's probably okay."

"You think so?"

"Yeah, I think it would be fine."

"Yeah."

"I mean, you already wrote it."

"That's true."

"So you might as well use it."

"Right."

"Right."

"Or maybe I will delete it."

"That would be okay too."

"REMEMBER THAT GOLDFISH I had?"

"I do. What did you call that thing?"

"Ronald Reagan."

"Are you sure?"

"I'm sure."

"How long did you have it for?"

"Just a few months."

"Didn't you drop a bowling ball on it, or something?"

"That happened. I dropped a bowling ball on it. But that is not what killed it."

"Really? What finally did it in?"

"I took it home with me for Thanksgiving break from college. The trip was just too much for the poor fuckface."

"The holidays are rough."

"I THINK I have gotten way too into wearing sandals."

"You will get over it once it starts to get cold."

"I don't know about that."

"Trust me. There is no such thing as snow sandals."

"Not yet anyway."

"Not ever."

"I'm the type that gets really obsessive about this sort of thing. I like to make things happen."

"I know you do. You slept in your sandals last night, after you had sex in your sandals, which happened right after you cried while wearing those God damn sandals."

"You need to be more supportive of this whole sandal thing."

"I'll try. But I want you to remember. The devil gives us things so we can be our worst selves. God takes things away so we can be our best selves."

"When did you get so biblical?"

"I can't remember. Maybe in another life."

"What were you in your last life?"

"A cave person. Or maybe an old person."

"Or a pine tree."

"Or a tampon."

"I think we were both tampons in another life."

"Or a jellyfish."

"I think I was definitely a storm cloud in my past life."

"No way."

"Then what do you think I was."

"I think you were a rabbit."

"A rabbit?"

"Yes, a rabbit with a big fluffy butt."

"I WOULD RATHER have permanent herpes of the butt and wiener than have my dog die."

"Yeah, obviously. But you shouldn't say stuff like that out loud."

"Why not?"

"People are going to think you want to get herpes."

"No. I just don't want to have a dead dog."

"Your dog's not dead."

"I also don't have herpes. Yet."

"Wait, I thought you weren't going to write about this."

"About what?"

"Our dog potentially having cancer."

"Well, I wasn't going to. You are the one that had to bring it up."

"But you wrote what I had said. You could have changed it."

"Shit, this is getting too heady."

"IT'S DEAD."

"You killed it."

"I'm a murderer."

"Poor moth."

"That bug had so much yellow stuff inside it."

"Maybe it ate a bunch of mustard. Maybe it was a mustard fiend. My uncle used to eat too much mustard even though the doctors told him it's bad for his pooping."

"I love mustard too."

"I love spicy mustard."

"Or mustard with horseradish in it."

"I remember when I was in camp there was this massive moth on the mirror in the bathroom and I killed it and my counselor, this skinny British guy, got so mad at me."

"For killing a bug?"

"He yelled at me. I mean, he really went off."

"What did he say?"

"I can't remember. But holy shit, he was mad."

"Did he hate you?"

"Maybe. I remember he would get really defensive when we would talk about the Revolutionary War."

"Why?"

"Because he's British. Or was. Maybe he's dead now."

"Do all British people get defensive about the Revolutionary War?"

"I doubt it."

"But he did?"

"Yeah, he said that they let us win and they were glad to have gotten rid of us."

"That's interesting."

"He said they lost on purpose."

"He was a sore loser, wasn't he?"

"I guess so."

"Remember when you met my grandma?"

"That was fun."

"Was it?"

"Sure. She was so old and stuck up and she had a harp. I didn't even know harps were actual real things."

"They are really. So real."

"And we played Scrabble."

"She kicked your ass."

"She really did."

"She kicked it hard."

"So hard."

"So fucking hard."

"And she recited that Auden poem to me."

"I remember that. Didn't you recite a poem too?"

"Sort of."

"What do you mean?"

"I'm really bad at memorizing things. So I just made the poem up."

"Holy shit. Really?"

"Yeah, I made the shit up."

"That's fucking nuts."

"I was really stoned at the time."

"You made up the poem on the spot?"

"Yeah."

"Do you think she could tell?"

"No. She had no idea."

"My grandma's been dead for a while now."

"Not really. Just a few years."

"That's a while."

"No, it's not. That's not long at all."

"It feels like a long time to me."

"Are you sad that you missed her funeral?"

"No. Not really."

"Funerals aren't important."

"Did you go to your grandma's funeral?"

"I did."

"Was it nice?"

"Not really."

"Do you wish you skipped it?"

"No, we went to Olive Garden afterwards."

"The Olive Garden? Really?"

"I got really drunk."

"How drunk?"

"Like frat boy level drunk."

"No..."

"I was fucking plastered."

"How many beers did you drink at the fucking Olive Garden?"

"So many. I thought everyone was getting drunk. But then I noticed that nobody else was even drinking beer."

"That's kinda sweet."

"I CAN'T BELIEVE this."

"Neither can I."

"Our puppy doesn't have cancer."

"I'm so relieved."

"We should celebrate."

"We should do something fun."

"Let's go for a drive."

"No. Not another drive."

"What's wrong?"

"I don't think I like driving as much as I used to."

"But driving is the cornerstone of this marriage."

"I know. Don't guilt trip me so much. I just don't like driving around aimlessly so much anymore. I've changed. I can't help that."

"Okay."

"You look upset."

"I'm fine."

"No you're not."

"It's true. I'm upset."

"Why?"

"It's really upsetting."

"Stop."

"When we first met we used to go for drives all the time. And now... you've changed."

"Listen, it's not like I won't ever go for a drive again. We will still go for drives. I just don't like it as much as I used to."

"What should we do instead?"

"We could get Amish cheese in Richfield Springs."

"I love Amish cheese."

"It's amazing stuff."

"And I love how those old bearded dudes ride around in those weird scooters."

"They know what they are doing."

"They really do."

"Let's go get some of that Amish cheese."

"But that's like forty minutes away. We will have to drive."

"I know."

"This is all really confusing."

"That's good. It should be confusing."

"WHEN WE DIE, do you think there's a heaven or do you think there is just nothingness?"

"I think heaven and nothingness are the same thing."

"What do you mean?"

"Think about it. What does everyone want to have happen when they die? What does everyone want heaven to be like?"

"A place where you are allowed to eat as much ice cream as you want."

"Right, ice cream. And what else?"

"I don't know."

"Most people want to see all their dead loved ones again. To be reunited with all they have lost."

"That's true."

"What is the most important part of hanging out with someone?"

"Laughing at jokes and being supportive and loving and stuff."

"Sure, that's true. But I think what we really want, what is most important to us is experiencing something with someone else. Experiencing something alone feels isolating and sad. So we like to experience things with other people. When we die, we experience the same nothingness as all our dead ones. Which means, in a way, we are experiencing it with them. We are hanging out with them. We are reunited by us all experiencing the same painless, simple nothingness."

"I can't tell if you are being pretentious or not?"

"Oh, trust me, I'm being really pretentious right now."

"So this is what you believe?"

"Part of me believes that. A big part of me. The other part of me thinks we have no business planning for the afterlife like it's a vacation."

"Or like it's retirement."

"Or like it's a spa."

"Or like it's summer camp."

"Or like it's a beach resort."

"Oh man, I wish heaven was like Popham, Maine, with all you can eat lobster bisque and blueberry ice cream."

"I think heaven is hippie girls being loud and walking around the woods stoned with me. Maybe showing me their butts occasionally."

"I'm kinda like that. I show you my butt."

"Kinda."

"What the fuck? I show you my butt all the time!"

"It's just not the same."

"You are such a dick."

"I'm sorry. I love your butt. I just think heaven will involve new butts. Butts I have never seen before."

"When I die I want to be cremated. What do you want done with that dumpy body of yours?"

"I want to just be dumped in the ground, naked, no coffin."

"That's not even legal."

"Sure it is."

"No, it's not."

"I checked. It's completely legal."

"It is?"

"Yup."

"Baby... I'm not doing that for you."

"You better. It's my dying wish."

"No way in hell I'm ever doing that shit. I'm going to cremate you. And scatter you all over Maine."

"Maine?"

"Yup. Maine."

"That's my least favorite place."

"Be nice, that's where I grew up."

"You know I hate Maine."

"Yeah. 'Cause you never shut up about it."

"But you brought it up."

"So, I have been feeling a little homesick."

"You have been homesick?"

"Yeah."

"Shit. I'm sorry. I didn't mean to rag on Maine so bad."

"It's okay."

"Some of Maine is nice. The ocean is big and cold. I like Baxter State Park. Stephen King lives there. That's pretty great."

"I miss Tu Casas in Portland."

"Me too."

"I wish we could eat there right now."

"Worst service. Best food."

"I miss their fried plantains."

"They were perfect."

"WE SHOULD BECOME monks."

"Both of us?"

"Yeah. Let's just forget about rent and dieting and car payments and family crap and everything and just wander around the woods wearing robes, trying not to think about things too much."

"Would we be allowed to have sex?"

"I don't know."

"What about our dog?"

"Shit. Can dogs be monks?"

"I don't think so. I doubt they are allowed at a monk house, or whatever they are called."

"You're right. They probably are not allowed in a 'monk house'."

"Wait, what kind of monks would we be? Christian or Buddhist or something else?"

"I don't even care anymore. I'm not ditching my dog, and I really like having sex with you."

"Ah, that's sweet. You need to put lotion in your mustache by the way, it's getting flaky."

"I HATE THE holidays. I really, really hate them."

"Oh no."

"I hate them so much. I hate them with the fiery passion of a bunch of fires."

"Not this again."

"I'm tired of the God damn holidays, ya hear me."

"Will you relax? It's the middle of summer. There are no holidays in sight."

"What about Fourth of July?"

"That was a week ago and we didn't even do anything because our dog was sick."

"I remember. We took care of our sick dog."

"Yes, we did."

"And that's a good thing to do. Taking care of sick dogs is good."

"Yes. Of course it is."

"I love our dog. Probably too much."

"We both do. But we did get to see fireworks from out the windows though. Remember? It was really nice."

"I agree. It was nice. But I still hate the holidays."

"I know you do."

"I hate them so much."

"Here we go."

"I love our dog. But I hate the holidays."

"I know. I know."

"I also hate fancy shoes. I only like sneakers. Old sneakers. Sneakers that have been in puddles, God damn it!"

"THE MOVIE THEATER is too old and loveable. It looks like the ghost of a Trapper Keeper in there."

"And it's cold even in the summer."

"So cold."

"I like the diner."

"Which one?"

"The one with the bathrooms."

"Oh, that one."

"That diner has the best bathrooms."

"Very handicap accessible for all the old people that eat there."

"I prefer the bathroom at Gilbert Lake state park. It makes me feel like I'm at summer camp."

"I like to drink wine at Hill City Grill."

"Me too. But I also like driving around and finding tiny churches in moldy towns surrounded by goldenrod."

"I love watching you cry. It makes me laugh."

"I like making you watch old and boring things."

"We might become old and boring together."

"We shouldn't have kids until we are like ninety years old."

"I can't wait to be the oldest parents ever."

"I don't want to have kids until I'm senile."

"As soon as that kid is born, it will have to take care of us."

"It will have to change our diapers."

"Amen."

"I GOT JOB ideas."

"Are they ways to make us rich?"

"I'm going to walk dogs for a living and buy scratch off tickets and then have the dogs scratch the scratch off tickets for me. That way I can scratch so many scratch off tickets."

"That's very industrious of you."

"I know. I'm a go-getter."

"Maybe you should go back to college though. Get that diploma. People love diplomas."

"Can you get a diploma in dog walking or scratch off tickets?"

"Probably not."

"Then it's not for me."

"When will my beard grow back?"

"It's coming. Be patient."

"The fucking thing is taking too long to grow. What if it doesn't grow enough ever and I'm stuck with this creepy, beady eyed, stepdad face."

"You look fine."

"I look like I manage a FYE."

"A what?"

"I look like a science teacher."

"Oh, stop."

"I look like a turkey with elephantiasis of the face."

"Okay, now that's just adorable."

"I hate my jowls."

"Stop."

"I'm ugly."

"I like your face. Your jowls are adorable."

"Married-people-love is so upsetting sometimes."

"Shut up, you love married love."

"I do. I need it a lot of the time."

"You really do."

"But don't you get it? I want to be a fucking sex symbol! Or at least not completely annoying looking."

"You look fine. You want to go to the bedroom and do stuff?"

"Naked?"

"Well, a little naked. Naked enough."

"How naked exactly?"

"I might keep my socks on."

"Socks are fine."

"Or maybe I'll keep my shirt on."

"I want you to take your shirt off."

"I might just roll it up and make it look like a belly shirt."

"Sounds like a fool proof plan to me."

"How's your dad?"

"Ummm."

"What's wrong?"

"I did something."

"What? What did you do?"

"Well, it's more like I didn't do something."

"Dear God, tell me. I can't handle this suspense."

"I forgot his birthday."

"No."

"I did. I forgot it. I forgot it completely."

"Is he mad?"

"I can't tell. He was laughing at me. He seemed to think it was funny. Oh man. This isn't good. He's going to hold this over my head for a long time."

"He really is."

"I'm fucked."

"He forgot your birthday once. And you have been guilt tripping him for years about it."

"I was just guilt tripping him about it a week ago. I can't do that anymore. The tides have turned. I can't use that trump card anymore."

"In a way forgetting his birthday is the best present you could have given him."

"It is. But I still feel really bad about it."

"I know."

"You know another bad thing about this?"

"What?"

"You forgot too."

"No."

"You did."

"Did I?"

"Yes."

"Oh shit. I did. God damn it."

"I LIKE FLOWERS now."

"I know you do."

"I see a house surrounded by flowers and I want to give that house a thumbs up, because I'm so happy about seeing the flowers. I just think it's a great fucking thing."

"You really are your father's son."

"Flowers are so sassy looking."

"They really are."

"They look ready to do stuff."

"Sexual stuff?"

"The most sexual stuff. All sorts of positions too."

"They have been known to pollinate."

"Baby, I'm not in my sexual prime anymore, and I want to apologize to you about that."

"It's okay. Really. I don't mind a bit."

"Pine trees, dude."

"For real."

"So many."

"They make shade."

"Shade for everyone."

"And for naps."

"So peaceful."

"No."

"No?"

"Bugs."

"Right."

"Summer bugs."

"They nibble."

"Nibble party!"

"Nonstop nibbling."

"Itchy."

"Still."

"Pine trees."

"Good."

"Favorite nature thing."

"Really?"

"Pine trees and creeks."

"And mossy rocks."

"And summer time girl butts."

"And picnics."

"Summer time guy butts."

"More summer things, please."

"Weed."

"And muddy sneakers."

"And storm clouds."

"And sunburns."

"And air conditioning."

"And naps."

"And dogs panting."

"And ice cream stands."

"Soft serve."

"Yard sales."

"Swampy crotches."

"Frogs."

"Car rides."

"Too many cars."

"Vacations."

"Hissy fits."

"Rashes."

"Sunburns."

"Mesh hats."

"Carnivals."

"Hot dogs."

"Can't leave the dog in the car."

"Nope."

"Nope."

"Wait."

"What?"

"More stuff."

"Okay."

"Goldenrod."

"Swimming with a shirt on."

"Crayfish."

"Mud."

"Weed."

"IPAs."

"No college kids."

"None."

"Porches."

"Old people."

"Cheese plates."

"Assorted cheeses."

"Ice coffee."

"Your dad's birthday."

"Pine cones."

"Tents."

"Fruit flies."

"Bug strips."

"Death."

"So much death."

"Families arguing outside the baseball hall of fame."

"Forever."

"It's an eternal thing."

"WE NEED TO be more fucking adorable."

"I agree."

"No more fucking around."

"Zero fucking around."

"We need to wear matching outfits."

"All day every day."

"When I wear yellow, you better fucking wear yellow."

"What about other colors, like green or pink or rainbow?"

"Same goes for all colors ever."

"Okay."

"No fucking around."

"None."

"None."

"We also need to take pictures of us sitting in front of a fireplace. A little fireplace. Maybe we could snuggle on carpet or something."

"WHAT THE FUCK is this?"

"It's a bed."

"A bed?"

"I made it all nice for us."

"This is what you call making a bed?"

"Yeah."

"Are you on drugs?"

"Do vitamins count as drugs?"

"This bed looks like a piece of shit. The blankets look all bunched up."

"C'mon..."

"Only an asshole would sleep in a bed like this."

"I like it. I think it looks worn in."

"This doesn't even count as anything."

"I think it counts."

"It does not count."

"Everything counts."

"This bed sucks ass."

"It's a good bed."

"It looks like a deer bed."

"Is that bad?"

"I just don't know anymore."

"Yes you do."

"I want a normal well-made bed. I want the blankets to be tucked in nicely, not all bunched up. I want a nice looking place. I want a normal looking place."

"I know you do."

"Stop making me feel bad for wanting nice things."

"What are you trying to say?"

"You are so frustrating."

"But I made the bed."

"But you made it badly."

"I think that's a matter of opinion."

"AHHHHHHHHHHHHHHHHHHHHHHHHH!"

"Do YOU BELIEVE in soul mates?"
    "Fuck you."

"CHECK OUT THIS meme."

"Holy shit, that is cute."

"It's so cute. It makes me feel rage."

"All I want to do is protect that picture."

"At all fucking costs."

"I'd protect it more though. 'Cause I'm generally more protective."

"You mean paranoid."

"Some say tomato, some say (insert fart noise here)."

"THE CARD WAS declined again."

"That sucks."

"I hate this card. It always gets declined."

"That card sucks."

"It needs more money in it."

"No. That card needs an exorcism."

"A reverse exorcism."

"Or a little bit of a double snuggle."

"Why is our card being so insecure?"

"Don't know. Maybe it's always been insecure. And we are just now noticing it. Poor thing."

"Have we been neglecting it? Have we been taking it for granted?"

"Maybe. Hard to tell."

"Our card needs a therapist."

"Or just a good cry."

"Our card needs a beer."

"No. It's already had too many beers."

"Beers can't help it now."

"Hmmm."

"They could help. Maybe."

"I get drunk after like two beers."

"Me too."

"Then I'm hungover halfway into my third."

"That's rough."

"I kinda like our card all moneyless."

"I don't."

"I think it gives it character."

"I think our card needs a healthier diet."

"A money diet?"

"You're darn tootin'."

"I WANT TO be better with money."

"I don't know what that means."

"We are broke."

"Right."

"We are always broke."

"That's true."

"We can't pay our bills."

"What's your point?"

"I want to be more on top of things, financially."

"I'd be careful if I were you."

"What do you mean?"

"People who are good with money are usually kinda depressing."

"That does seem true a lot of the time."

"Or I could be really delusional."

"About what?"

"Money."

"Am I delusional?"

"Can't tell."

"Hey! Watch this!"

"Oh God."

"Where did my pants go! They disappeared!"

"You are ridiculous."

"I can't find my pants. And we can't afford new pants. What am I going to do?"

"Take a fucking shower?"

"Hey, what are you trying to say?"

"That your balls smell like never ending war over oil."

"That's good though. Right?"

"No, it's sad. It could ruin the environment."

"Are my sweaty dodge balls responsible for global warming?"

"Hard to tell. The science isn't conclusive. But. Maybe."

"You NEED TO apologize."

"Why?"

"Because you were grumpy when I came home."

"I was grumpy because you were rude."

"I wasn't THAT rude."

"Well, I wasn't THAT grumpy."

"You were very grumpy and it hurt my feelings."

"You hurt my feelings first."

"This isn't a competition."

"Yes it is."

"No it's not."

"It so is."

"No. It isn't."

"You hurt my feelings first."

"So?"

"So, you don't get to hurt my feelings then have ME apologize for getting my feelings too hurt."

"That's not what I did."

"Yes it is."

"I'm hungry now."

"Me too."

"Should we get pizza from Nina's?"

"Let's do it."

"And should we continue fighting when we get to the pizza place?"

"Once I eat, I probably won't be grumpy anymore."

"Ha. That's the real reason you're grumpy, isn't it?"

"Shit."

"You are just grumpy from hunger. I knew it was something like that."

"Ummm."

"Now you really do owe me an apology."

"I'm sorry."

"Thank you. That was a very good apology."

"You are very welcome."

"I LOVE THE crunchy stuff in eggs."

"That's the shell."

"It is?"

"Oh shit."

"WE SHOULD OPEN our own bed and breakfast."

"In our tiny little apartment?"

"It's a good gimmick. People from all over the world would come to stay in our crusty little apartment. They would pay big bucks to sleep on our smelly mattresses, and piss in our bathroom, which is the size of an airplane bathroom."

"And don't forget our kitchen where you can't have more than one person in it without someone getting stabbed or burned."

"And our crappy furniture."

"Only the crappiest for us."

"Exactly. It would be a lot of fun."

"I LIKE OUR place."

"Me too."

"I think we should show more pride in it."

"This is pride."

"Is it?"

"I think so."

"I think we shouldn't be so hard on it."

"I like making fun of things. I think it's a very loving thing to do."

"This place is nice."

"I never said it wasn't."

"We have a big back yard and our dog rolls around on her back in the short grass and it's very pleasant."

"It's a great back yard. We have pine trees and shade."

"It's great. It's why I wanted to live here."

"I'm just glad we don't live in our car."

"I hate sleeping in cars."

"It's not comfortable."

"Not at all."

"I LIKE THE public pool but sometimes I get to staring at people in their bathing suits looking all wedgied and round and muscular and saucy looking and I feel bad for myself. And for them too, 'cause they can see me staring. It's a problem."

"You should wear sunglasses."

"That's a good call."

"Or get your eyes plucked out."

"That is a great idea too. We could sell them to some crazed eye pervert in Delaware. Make some money. Go on some vacations."

"Why Delaware?"

"Why not? It seems like a decent place. A little needy."

"Needy?"

"It needs some attention. And it knows it."

"So true. Delaware needs some consistent pervert love."

"It's the most true form of love."

"Are you crying?"

"I might be."

"You are crying."

"I gotta cry a lot."

"Why?"

"It's how I sustain myself."

"Crying helps sustain you?"

"It does. It really does."

"Pizza sustains you too though."

"Pizza is almost as good as crying."

"I USED TO pee my pants a lot, when I was a kid."

"I figured."

"It was easy enough."

"I can imagine."

"You ever pee your pants?"

"Nope."

"Even when you were young?"

"Unlike you, I was a potty trained child."

"Except for the time you peed in the corner of your dorm room."

"Did that happen?"

"Oh yeah. Junior year."

"I don't know about that."

"That was the year we fell in love."

"I remember that part."

"One day you got drunk and peed in the corner of your dorm room."

"Okay, now I remember."

"There ya go."

"That was a good night."

"Night? You were passed out by 4 p.m."

"All the best nights end at 4 p.m."

"All the best pants have been peed in."

"So true."

"DID YOU LIKE living in New York?"

"I did. I got drunk and kissed strangers."

"Why did you leave?"

"The parks in the city seemed too sad and mutated and sickly. Trees looked like weeds. There were swans with legs growing out of their buttholes. At night, as I ate dollar pizza from Kennedy Fried Chicken, I would see armies of rats running around the short grass."

"Gross."

"Totally."

"Was it loud there?"

"It was very loud. Sometimes living in the city was like living in a mall."

"It would be fun to visit there someday."

"It really would be."

"WHEN I WAS young, we used to pull down each other's pants. It was a fun thing to do. We called it pantsing."

"I imagine it's still fun."

"One time someone pantsed my buddy Jon. His underwear came down with his pants and everyone saw his peter pumpkin eater."

"His what?"

"His dick. Everyone saw his dick. And he was humiliated. Which is normal. You are supposed to be humiliated by that sort of thing. That's what makes it so funny. But then everybody felt bad for him. So they got together and agreed not to tease him about it."

"That was nice of them."

"I thought it sucked."

"Why?"

"'Cause they wouldn't have done that for me. Or any of the other crustier kids."

"I think they would have."

"Ah, what do you know?"

"I know, when I met you, you liked to pull your own pants down at parties and you didn't care if people were laughing AT you or WITH you. You just liked it when people laughed."

"What are you saying?"

"I'm saying you need to be less bitter."

"Is this foreplay? Are you trying to hook up with me?"

"No, not at all."

"I USED TO go to clubs and dance. It was great exercise. And sometimes you got to kiss a stranger."

"Did you dress hip and fancy?"

"I tried."

"And?"

"Well, I wore oversized sweaters and button ups my mom had bought me for church when I was a teenager. I looked more like Garrison Keillor than the other guys at the club."

"Did you twerk?"

"Twerking hadn't been invented yet. We had this other thing called grinding. Which was just dry humping."

"We should go to a club and do that."

"No, it was the worst. Spending so much time in clubs is one of the few things I regret in life."

"What are the other things?"

"The other things I regret? Well, I shaved my eyebrows once when I was twelve. And I didn't go to my friend Aaron's funeral. And I was really mean to this one girl I dated. And I made you wait seven years before we bought a dog. And I wish we hadn't ever moved out of Astoria, Oregon. And I wish I knew how to play basketball. I wish I had never gotten fat. And I wish my mom was still around to yell at me about stuff."

"Your mom liked to yell?"

"She was really, really good at it."

"I wish I could have met her. We could yell at you together."

"That would have been nice."

"EVERYTHING COUNTS."

"Stop. I know you heard that in that Sam Shepard documentary and you think it's SO profound. But it isn't."

"It's profound enough for me."

"Oh god..."

"You're projecting onto me again."

"No way, you are projecting onto me."

"Fuck off. This is a projection of your issues. You have projected onto me and it's not fair."

"Umm, I know a projection when I see one and this is definitely a high level of projection of YOUR bullshit, not mine."

"Wait, what if we have projected both our issues at the same time and these projections have somehow created a weird conjoined marriage monster who is constantly projecting its own issues onto itself?"

"Nice idea. Really unique. But I'm pretty sure this is just you projecting your issues onto me."

"I think all this bickering is scaring the dog."

"Or just annoying her."

"Or maybe our sweet puppy is just really entertained."

"No, she's annoyed, trust me."

"Holy shit, we got really sunburned."

"Sunburned to the max."

"The maxiest."

"How did this happen? I mean, we hike all the time. We never get this sunburned."

"We were hiking with family this time. They left us vulnerable both emotionally and physically."

"That's stupid."

"Is it?"

"Maybe there was a hole in the atmosphere."

"And we got caught in it and now we are crispy lobster people."

"Or maybe it was just really sunny."

"Don't make me do it."

"Oh stop."

"I'm going to run away. I'm going to run away from home."

"Seriously. You're being a dick face."

"I've done it before. I'll take our mattress with me and build a fort in the woods and it will be so hidden and secret you will never find me."

"I'll find you. And I'll yell at you for leaving me."

"Nope. I'll be too busy sleeping with models. Maybe I'll become a model expert and make more than enough money to afford my own fort in the woods for all eternity."

"Or you could just do the dishes every once in a while. That would solve a lot of our issues."

"The dishes?"

"Yup."

"All of them?"

"All of them."

"Are you kidding? My fingers will get pruney."

"I like pruney fingers."

"Do you?"

"I think they are sexy."

"Stop harassing me. I'm sensitive."

"Mmmmmmm."

"I just want to be a runway model."

"I know you do, baby."

"Stop being so supportive. It's horrible."

"LISTEN BUTT FACE. These dialogue poems I'm writing are going to save our marriage."

"Shut up. Our marriage is fine."

"These poems are going to save everyone's marriage. Soon every day will feel like a long make-out session with a stranger. And it will feel this way for everyone. All the time. Forever."

"Or Trump will become president and make things so awful we will have to hide in the woods and make a fort and become awkward beasts, and we will forget about poetry and watching TV and taking pictures of trees with our cell phones, and we will finally be free."

"Or maybe we will just start writing our poems on rock faces and boulders like that ancient Chinese mountain poet, Han Shan. Also known as Cold Mountain."

"Didn't that dude drink a lot of wine?"

"Lots and lots of wine."

"Okay, I'm down."

"Down with what?"

"The thing."

"What thing?"

"You know, the thing."

"Wait. What are we talking about?"

"It's starting to thunder."

"This air conditioning is so old and loud."

"I don't mind it."

"You don't mind any noise though. You sleep so easily. It's creepy to me."

"I've always slept well."

"This fucking machine is making so much noise I can't stand it."

"I think it's pleasant."

"I usually think so too. I usually love the sweet hum of an air conditioner turned on full blast. But this one sounds messed up. It sounds like it has indigestion."

"At least you can't hear the train or the drunk college kids."

"The college kids are all home for the summer."

"Right. I almost forgot."

"I hate the college kids."

"Me too."

"It's amazing how much more likeable this town is once the college kids are gone."

"Everyone's so friendly now."

"It's true. Everyone's constantly waving hello and smiling."

"The old people in the house across the street spend all day hanging out and eating cheese and crackers. It's just cheese and crackers all day every day."

"I didn't even know anyone lived there."

"Me neither."

"I thought the house was abandoned."

"I guess they were just hiding from college kids."

"It must be so weird to be old and see college kids partying and acting sleazy."

"I bet it's lonely."

"If I was old I would want to go and party every once in a while."

"Imagine if you got drunk then you woke up with a ninety-year-old in your bed."

"What if one day they cure oldness?"

"Who's they?"

"Them."

"Who?"

"The people who invent stuff."

"Scientists?"

"Doctors and stuff."

"Right."

"I'm just saying. It could happen. They could cure oldness."

"Like nobody would die of just getting old or any of that old people stuff."

"Exactly."

"Shit, that would be awful."

"You think so?"

"Yeah. It's a good thing to fade away like that. It's awkward, but good."

"I just don't like the idea of peeing myself all the time."

"I like the idea of taking my time to get ready to die."

"But are you ever TRULY ready to die, even when you are really saggy and old?"

"Maybe not. But it would be good to just try. To try and be ready. That seems like an important thing to do."

"I guess being prepared for death, or at least giving it some rehearsal time, is a noble thing to do."

"And besides, I want to get old. I want to be the kind of old person that's really goofy and gives really bad advice."

"That would be great."

"It would be the best. Hang out on a front porch. Drink a diet soda. Wave hello to people. Give bad advice. Sounds like the best time ever."

"You should give me bad advice."

"I already do that."

"No you don't."

"Fuck off. I give you bad advice all the time."

"No, your advice is pretty solid."

"You never give me any credit."

"Yes, I do."

"No, you don't. I've been paying close attention to the amount of credit you have been giving me, and trust me, the amount of credit you have been dealing my way on any given day, has been very, very scant indeed."

"'INDEED?' You use the word INDEED nowadays?"

"I have been watching a lot of *Downton Abbey*."

"Without me?"

"Uh oh."

"What the fuck's wrong with you?"

"HEATHER GRIMBOL, COME to bed, I have to tell you something."

"Just one second."

"Jesus, could you hurry please?"

"Don't rush me."

"Please come to bed, I have to tell you something really important."

"Relax."

"I won't relax."

"Okay, I'm in bed. What do you want to tell me?"

"I have to tell you something."

"I know. What is it?"

"I want to be a good person."

"Shut up."

"No, I'm serious. I don't want to be fancy or vain or conceited."

"Well, you don't have to worry about being fancy."

"I don't want to be clever or too intelligent. I just want to be sincere. I want to be helpful."

"Like maybe doing the laundry with me tomorrow?"

"No, not that helpful. But helpful. And I want to drive around and love what everything looks like. And I want to hike up mountains and not get too chafed. And, every once in a while, I want to go down on you until you are finished."

"You could do that right now."

"Stop, I'm being serious."

"So am I."

"I want to be good to you and have kids with you and live in a small house that needs lots of maintenance. I want to live in Vermont and visit the place where we met."

"You are so cheesy."

"I know."

"Well, you know what I want?"

"What?"

"I want to go camping this weekend."

"Where? We could travel up to Canada, or leave really early and go up to the Upper Michigan Peninsula. Or we can go to the Badlands. Or we can just quit everything and drive around the country."

"Let's just go to Vermont."

"I could sell all these old books to Hermit Hill books in Poultney."

"We could camp at Lake St. Catherine."

"We need to buy a blow up mattress."

"That's true. The ground is way too hard."

"And filled with dead people."

Justin Grimbol lives in Westminster West, Vermont, with his wife and dog.

Other **Atlatl Press** Books

We Did Everything Wrong by C.V. Hunt

Squirm With Me by Andersen Prunty

Hard Bodies by Justin Grimbol

Arafat Mountain by Mike Kleine

Drinking Until Morning by Justin Grimbol

Thanks For Ruining My Life by C.V. Hunt

Death Metal Epic (Book One: The Inverted Katabasis)
by Dean Swinford

Fill the Grand Canyon and Live Forever by Andersen Prunty

Mastodon Farm by Mike Kleine

Fuckness by Andersen Prunty

Losing the Light by Brian Cartwright

They Had Goat Heads by D. Harlan Wilson

The Beard by Andersen Prunty

www.ingramcontent.com/pod-product-compliance
Lightning Source LLC
Chambersburg PA
CBHW031537040426
42445CB00010B/585